THE APOSTLE PAUL

TODD WILSON

Paul's Life and Background

Paul's Letters

Paul's Theology

Paul's Legacy

Paul the Man

River bank, Tarsus.

The apostle Paul is undoubtedly one of the most influential figures in human history. He also happens to be one of the most enigmatic and controversial. Over the years, some have claimed that Paul was the real founder of Christianity, and others that he actually corrupted the pristine faith of Jesus and his earliest followers. For some, Paul remained a faithful Jew even after his conversion, while others think that his call to preach to the Gentiles marked a clean break with his past. So, when thinking about the apostle Paul, we encounter a complex and fascinating figure.

Paul's background

One of our earliest descriptions of Paul (albeit of limited historical value) is that he was 'a man of small stature, with a bald head and crooked legs, in a good state of body, with eyebrows meeting and a nose somewhat hooked, full of friendliness' (*Acts of Paul*, 3.1; see 2 Cor. 10:10).

As to his family, we know Paul had at least one sister, who lived in Jerusalem, and who had a son who helped Paul (Acts 23:16). And while some have speculated otherwise, it seems unlikely that Paul ever married or had children (see 1 Cor. 7:8).

Paul came from Tarsus, the capital city of Cilicia, and an important city politically, economically and militarily. It was, as Paul says, 'no ordinary city' (Acts 21:39, NIV), having received the patronage of the Caesars on more than one occasion. A city known for its love of learning, Tarsus stood at the intersection of two dominant cultures: the Greek east and the Roman west.

Paul was a Roman citizen, an important privilege he probably inherited from his parents. Roman citizenship gave Paul certain rights and protections unavailable to non-citizens, and these would have been particularly useful for him during his extensive travels. Acts tells us that Paul appealed to his Roman citizenship to help him negotiate his way through several difficult situations (see Acts 16:37–39; 22:25–29; 25:7–12).

Paul was also – and most importantly – a Jew, a fact to which he appeals at several strategic points in his letters. In his letter to the Philippians, for example, he provides a résumé of his Jewish heritage: 'circumcised on the eighth day, of the people of Israel, of the tribe of Benjamin, a Hebrew of Hebrews; as to the law, a Pharisee; as to zeal, a persecutor of the church; as to righteousness, under the law blameless' (Phil. 3:5–6; see Gal. 1:13–17; 1 Cor. 15:8–10; 2 Cor. 11:22; Rom. 11:1). Each of these phrases is significant for giving us a sense of Paul's cultural pedigree and background.

An old street in Tarsus.

Paul's education

Paul was brought up in Jerusalem and received his education there at the feet of a leading Jewish figure named Gamaliel (see Acts 22:3). He describes his education as 'according to the strict manner of the law of our fathers' (Acts 22:3; Gal. 1:14). This meant he would have devoted his time to mastering the Jewish scriptures, the Old Testament. In addition, Paul says he was zealous for those time-honoured ways of understanding and applying the Jewish scriptures: what he calls, 'the traditions of my fathers' (Gal. 1:14).

It is important to bear in mind that Paul was not just any kind of Jew, but trained in a particular tradition of Judaism. He was a Pharisee, with a Pharisee's devotion to the Law (Phil. 3:5). Pharisees were, as Paul acknowledges, one of the strictest sects of Judaism (Acts 26:5). They were, for example, very strict about ritual purity and the precise observance of the Jewish Law. This rigorous training, in turn, bred in Paul a zeal that made him want to protect the integrity of the Jewish faith at whatever cost to himself or others.

Paul's trade

How did Paul make a living? Unlike many today, Paul was bi-vocational. In addition to his missionary endeavours, he also practised another full-time job. He was, as Acts tells us an artisan. He was a 'tentmaker' (18:3; 20:34–35), which means that he was also a leather-worker, a skill he probably acquired during his educational training.

Financially, Paul was on a par with other manual labourers, and would have been able to generate only a modest income for himself. Even so, he prided himself on the fact that he laboured tirelessly, 'working with our own hands' (1 Cor. 4:12), so as not to be a financial burden on any of his churches (1 Thess. 2:9; 2 Thess. 3:8–9; 2 Cor. 6:5; 11:23; 1 Cor. 9:3–18). Though he had the right to receive remuneration for his service, Paul nevertheless preached the gospel 'free of charge' (1 Cor. 9:18).

Authentic scale model of Herod's Temple, Jerusalem, showing the various courtyards.

Paul's Conversion

Paul's pre-conversion persecutions

The hallmark of Paul's pre-conversion life in Judaism was his persecution of Christians (Gal. 1:13, 23; 1 Cor. 15:9; Phil. 3:6; Acts 22:4; 1 Tim. 1:13). This features prominently in Luke's account in Acts (8:3; 9:2; 22:4; 26:10–11).

But why did Paul persecute Christians? What did he find so offensive, and why did he take such extreme measures to 'destroy' the church of God (Gal. 1:13)? The impression we get is that his persecuting activity was the result of his extreme zeal for the 'tradition of my fathers' (Gal. 1:14; Phil. 3:5–6; Acts 22:3–4). Paul was a zealous Pharisee, who saw the early Christians' worship of a crucified and (evidently) accursed criminal (see Deut. 21:23; Gal. 3:13) as utterly scandalous (see 1 Cor. 1:17, 18, 23).

Paul also probably took offence at the way in which Jewish converts to Christianity came to treat the Jewish Law. While it is unlikely that Jewish converts would have completely abandoned their former way of life, we know that they would have had a different attitude towards the Law because of the work of Christ. They would have also changed their view of, and attitude towards, non-Jews (Gentiles). All this would have been explosive to a zealous Jew such as Paul.

Paul's confrontation with the risen Christ

Everything changed for Paul on the road to Damascus, when he was confronted by the Lord Jesus Christ, risen from the dead. Interestingly, the book of Acts recounts Paul's conversion on three separate occasions (Acts 9, 22, 26). Several things emerge from these retellings.

1. Paul's conversion entailed a specific call to take the gospel to the Gentiles. He was thus not only converted, but called – specifically set apart – to serve as Christ's

'chosen instrument' to carry his name before the Gentiles (Acts 9:15).
2. Paul was going to suffer greatly for the sake of the gospel. As the risen Lord says to Ananias: 'I will show him how much he must suffer for the sake of my name' (Acts 9:16). As both the shape of his life and the content of his letters reveal, Paul's ministry was defined by his commitment to endure hardship for the sake of the gospel among the Gentiles.

Paul's early preaching

Following his encounter with the risen Lord, Paul remained 'for some days' in Damascus, where he preached Christ in the local synagogues (Acts 9:19–20). This evidently met with some hostility, for Acts tells us that the Jews there now plotted to kill him (9:23). So Paul had to slip out of Damascus unnoticed (Acts 9:25; 2 Cor. 11:33), and from there went to Arabia (Gal. 1:17). The purpose and duration of Paul's stay in Arabia is uncertain, though we can imagine he continued to reflect upon the implications of his encounter with the risen Christ.

In any event, after three years Paul went up to Jerusalem and was there introduced to leading figures in the early church: Peter (or Cephas, his Aramaic name) and James, the Lord's brother (Gal. 1:18–19; cf. Acts 9:26–30). Then, after a short stay of only fifteen days, Paul went back to the town of his birth, Tarsus in Cilicia. There he was recruited by Barnabas to come to the church in Antioch in Syria (Acts 11:25–26; Gal. 1:21). Syrian Antioch then became Paul's strategic base of operations for his mission and ministry in the years to come.

A fourth-century fresco of St Paul from a catacomb in Rome.

Paul's Mission

How did Paul approach the task of evangelizing the nations? What was his strategy? A close look at his travels reveals that he tended to visit Roman provincial capitals and, for ease of movement, to travel along Roman roads. This was sensible, as well as convenient. It was also safer, since travel in the ancient world could be quite dangerous, and Paul travelled extensively – several thousand miles in total.

Paul was apparently driven by a specific vision for evangelizing the known world. We learn from his letter to the Romans, for example, that he understood himself to be a pioneer missionary and church-planter. As he says, he made it his ambition 'to preach the gospel, not where Christ has already been named, lest [he] build on someone else's foundation' (15:20). This impelled him in his missionary endeavours to move continually westwards 'from Jerusalem and all the way around to Illyricum' (Rom. 15:19), then to Rome and eventually even to Spain, which represented the outermost reaches of the known world.

Paul's chronology

Establishing a fixed chronology for Paul's life and letters is surprisingly difficult. For example, we do not know the exact date of Paul's birth, conversion or death. We do nevertheless have a fairly clear picture of the basic chronological outline of his life and ministry (see box on page 16). We can safely assume that Paul's conversion happened some time around A.D. 32 and was followed by roughly a decade of relative silence – a period about which we know very little.

Then, some time around A.D. 45, Paul embarked on the first of what were to be three great missionary journeys, spanning roughly a decade (A.D. 45–57), during which time he would also write most of the letters we now possess. While the precise date and circumstances surrounding Paul's death remain somewhat shrouded in mystery, it is likely that he was executed some time during the reign of the Emperor Nero, around A.D. 67.

Remains of a wide Roman street in ancient Antioch in Pisidia, visited by Paul on his first missionary journey.

Remains of ancient Perga.

Antalya, southern Turkey, ancient Attalia.

Following the outline in Acts, we know that Paul engaged in three major missionary journeys. These were concerted efforts to advance the gospel westwards into unevangelized, largely Gentile, territories.

The details of the first journey, which lasted a couple of years, are recorded in Acts chapters 13–14. Having been commissioned by the church in Antioch, Paul and Barnabas travelled first to Cyprus, and then into southern Asia Minor (present-day Turkey), evangelizing in cities such as Antioch in Pisidia, Lystra, Derbe and Iconium.

Paul's second journey, which penetrated into Macedonia and Greece, lasted about four years, eighteen months of which were spent in Corinth (Acts 16–18). Paul spent part of this journey revisiting some of the congregations he had founded on his first journey.

Paul's third journey similarly started from Antioch (Acts 18:23) and took him to Ephesus, where he spent as long as three years teaching and evangelizing (Acts 19). On his return, Paul went up to Jerusalem and was there arrested and eventually sent to Rome to stand trial before Caesar. This is where Acts rather unceremoniously ends (see Acts 21–28).

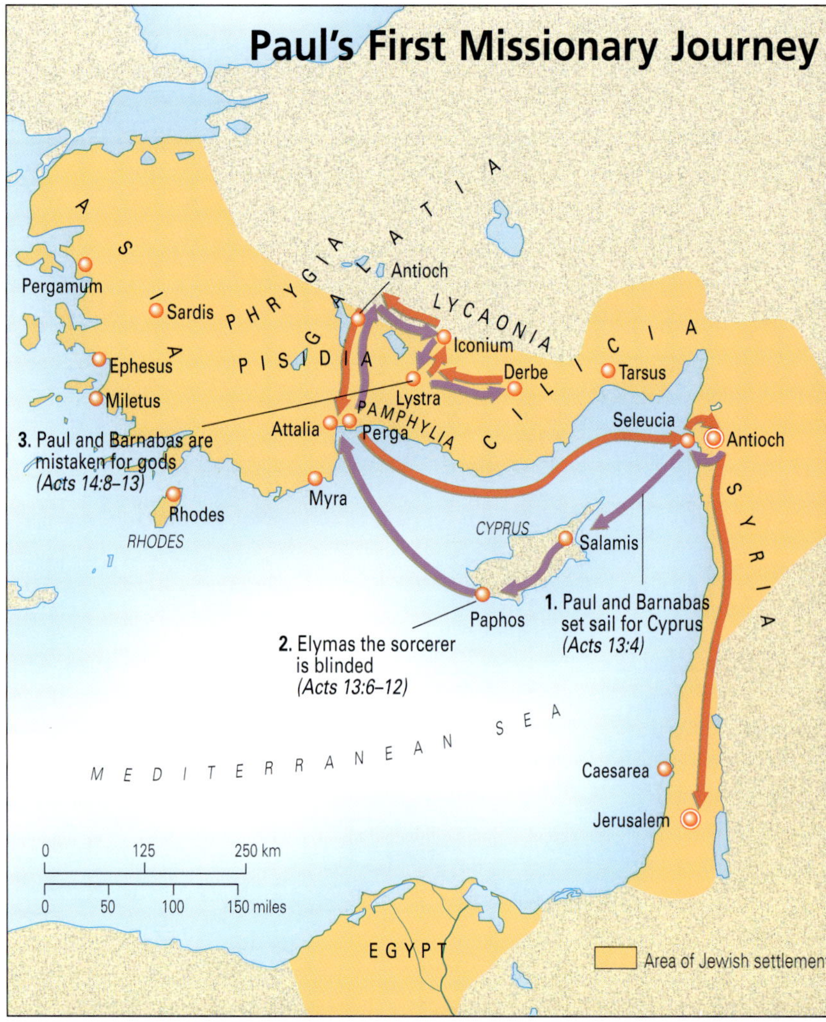

Paul's co-workers

Because we know Paul as a pioneer missionary, we sometimes imagine him as a solitary figure, working in isolation. The reality was quite different. Paul carried out his missionary endeavour in partnership with a network of co-workers.

Paul often refers to these co-workers by name, usually in the opening of his letters. Names include Sosthenes (1 Cor. 1:1), Timothy (2 Cor. 1:1) and Silvanus (1 Thess. 1:1). Elsewhere, Paul mentions Mark, Aristarchus, Demas and Luke, whom he calls 'my fellow workers' (Philemon 24). When addressing the Galatians, he refers simply to 'all the brothers who are with me' (1:2). This substantial network of Christian labourers was vital to the success of Paul's mission. They bolstered his ministry, visited his congregations (Phil. 2:19–30) and carried his letters (Eph. 6:21–22).

Remains of Roman aqueduct, Antioch in Pisidia.

The collection

An important aspect of Paul's ministry was a collection that he gathered from his Gentile converts for the Jewish believers in Jerusalem. This undertaking consumed a considerable amount of Paul's energy and time over a number of years, and it is clear that, from Paul's perspective, much depended upon the successful completion and delivery of this collection (see 1 Cor. 16.1–4; 2 Cor. 8–9; Rom. 15.25–32). It symbolized the unity of the early church, the basic accord between the Jewish and Gentile wings of Christianity. It also served as a token of Paul's continuing loyalty to the Jewish people – despite appearances to the contrary. So important was the collection that Paul was willing to risk his life for it (see Acts 20:22–24; 21:4–14).

An Impassioned Letter: Galatians

Galatians is Paul's most impassioned letter and reveals his deep concern for his churches and his absolute fidelity to what he calls 'the truth of the gospel' (2:14). We get a clear sense of Paul's dismay over what has happened in Galatia in 3:1: 'O foolish Galatians! Who has bewitched you? It was before your eyes that Jesus Christ was publicly portrayed as crucified.' At least in Paul's mind, things had gone terribly wrong in Galatia – and Paul's letter to the Galatians is his attempt to put things right.

Who were the Galatians?

While there is some debate as to the exact location of the Galatians, we have good reason to think that they comprised a number of small house-churches that Paul founded during his first missionary journey and that were located in the cities of Antioch in Pisidia, Lystra, Iconium and Derbe in the southern part of the Roman province of Galatia (see Acts 13–14).

If we accept this definition, then it follows that Paul probably wrote this letter shortly after his first missionary journey and just before the Jerusalem Council (see Acts 15), which would make Galatians perhaps Paul's earliest letter.

Why is Paul so angry?

It is clear from the opening verses of Galatians that Paul is deeply troubled by what has transpired within these churches: 'I am astonished that you are so quickly deserting him who called you in the grace of Christ and are turning to a different gospel' (1:6).

Paul is incensed by the influence of certain false teachers, who were

Mound at the site of ancient Colossae.

heralding 'another gospel' and leading the Galatians astray. These 'agitators', as Paul calls them, had infiltrated the Galatian churches and were evidently claiming that Paul's Gentile converts needed to be circumcised and perhaps embrace other aspects of the Jewish Law in order to be acceptable before God (see 5:1–4; 6:12–13).

Paul has harsh words for these troublemakers (see 4:17, 30; 5:12; 6:12–13). He is also distraught because the Galatians, by turning away from the true Pauline gospel, have put their own future in jeopardy. As Paul says: 'You observe days and months and seasons and years! I am afraid I may have laboured over you in vain' (4:10–11). The Galatians are threatening a fall from grace (5:4).

What is Galatians about?

At one level, Galatians is obviously about whether Gentile converts needed to embrace the Jewish Law and circumcision. Paul's answer, of course, is a resounding 'No'. And Paul devotes much of the letter to defending his case (2:15–3:29). But at another level, Galatians is about the

Remains of the Temple of Artemis (Diana) at Ephesus. This was once one of the Seven Wonders of the World, but today stands in a marsh.

Ephesus. View from the theatre towards the ancient port.

'truth of the gospel' (2:14) and the resulting profound reorientation of the order of things in light of the 'coming faith' (3:23) and the dawning of the 'new creation' (6:15).

But Galatians is not only about theology, it deals also with ethics. Paul is concerned not just with what the Galatians think, but with how they live. The letter reveals that the Galatians are no longer serving one another in love, but instead are engaged in all kinds of socially destructive behaviour that is undermining the integrity of their communities (see 5:15, 19–21, 26).

Paul uses a graphic image of the Galatians being in a dogfight with each other (5:15). Paul is concerned to call the Galatians back to a life of loving service, which, as he reminds them, is actually the fulfilment of the Law (5:14; see 6:2). This explains the prominence of the Spirit in the closing chapters of the letter, since only the Spirit can effect the fruit of love within the life of the Galatian churches (5:22–23).

A Joyful Letter – and its Sequel:
1 & 2 Thessalonians

Baths of Faustina, Miletus.

1 Thessalonians

1 Thessalonians is one of Paul's brightest letters. The believers gathered in the city of Thessalonica exuded such sincere faith, hope and love that all the surrounding regions were affected. Paul and Silvanus (Silas) first came to Thessalonica after having suffered in Philippi (Acts 16:11–24; 17:1–9).

By contrast to its reception in Philippi, in Thessalonica the message fell on receptive ears, particularly among the many devout Greeks and prominent women in the city (Acts 17:4). Remarkably, these new converts embraced opposition from the Jewish leadership, as well as from the civic authorities. Paul pens his first letter to the Thessalonians in this context, and takes the opportunity to express his gratitude to God for the reception and expansion of the gospel through them (gratitude: 1:2; 2:13; 3:9; expansion: 1:7–9; 2:14; 4:9–10).

1 Thessalonians is written in response to the joyful news of the Thessalonians' continued steadfastness of faith, as it had been reported to Paul by Timothy. Being hindered from visiting, Paul wrote to express his own exuberance (chs. 1–3), and to exhort them to continue in the faith (chs. 4–5).

1. Paul calls them to grow in their sanctification (4:1–12).
2. Paul informs them about the time and manner of Christ's second coming, applying it to those who have already passed away (4:13–5:11).
3. Paul challenges them to live sanctified lives with one another (5:12–22).

These exhortations are framed between two benedictions, which capture Paul's heart for the community (3:11–13; 5:23–24).

2 Thessalonians

Paul turns up the heat in 2 Thessalonians. Together with Silvanus and Timothy, Paul continues to be encouraged by the growth of faith and increase of love in the church in Thessalonica (1:3). The exhortations of the first letter had evidently been effective and resulted in continued obedience.

However, fresh persecution and the intensity of lawlessness has occasioned some false views about Christ's second coming and divine judgement (2:1–12). Therefore, Paul must clarify God's purposes for these new believers, and does so by highlighting the uniqueness of his apostolic authority and teaching (2:2–3, 5, 15; 3:4, 6–10, 17).

Arch of Galerius, ancient Thessalonica.

1. Paul assures the Thessalonian Christians of God's just and merciful purpose for suffering (1:4–12). Nothing less than the glory of the Lord Jesus Christ should be the hope and expectation of the believers (1:11–12). Likewise, nothing less than separation from Christ's glory will be the judgement and condemnation of the wicked (1:9).

Remains of the Roman theatre at Miletus.

2. Paul fortifies the mind and spirit of the Thessalonians by reassuring them of God's purpose for the Day of the Lord (2:1–12). While the present era abounds with evil and deception (2:7, 11), God's final victory in Christ is certain (2:10–12). These realities ought not only to fortify their faith but also comfort their hearts (2:17). Thus Paul challenges them to hold fast both to his apostolic teaching (2:13–17) and his apostolic character (3:6–15).

Letters to a Divided Church:

1 & 2 Corinthians

Our knowledge of ancient Corinth illuminates the issues Paul confronts in his two letters to the church there. Corinth was a prominent Roman city; its strategic location making it a crossroads socially, culturally and intellectually. In addition, Corinth had developed a somewhat notorious reputation for licentious living. One ancient Greek writer coined the expression 'to act like a Corinthian' as a way of referring to fornication.

1 Corinthians

1 Corinthians provides us with fascinating and invaluable insight into Paul's pastoral theology, that is, his approach to dealing with the various issues and problems in his churches in the light of his own beliefs about God and Christ, humanity and salvation. Interestingly, Paul says that he writes 1 Corinthians to 'remind' the Corinthians of his 'ways in Christ' (1 Cor. 4:17).

From the start, we see Paul's concern to address issues of factionalism and dissension within the Corinthian church. Apparently, members were identifying with this or that teacher in a way that encouraged divisions. We see throughout the letter Paul's concern to call the church in Corinth back to unity (1:10; 3:1–4; 4:14; 5:4; 6:1; 8:9; 10:17; 11:33–34).

The Temple of Apollo, Corinth, with Acrocorinth in the background.

A way of love

The Corinthian believers had evidently become inappropriately preoccupied with spiritual gifts, which, rather than being used to edify the body, had become grounds for boasting and sources of pride. Paul, however, will have nothing of it and proposes an alternative way: the way of love (1 Cor. 13).

The letter divides into two main sections: the first contains Paul's response to various issues in the church which he has heard about from 'Chloe's people' (1 Cor. 1:11). The second section provides Paul's direct response to several issues raised by the Corinthians in a previous letter, each issue introduced with the expression: 'Now concerning . . .' (7:1; 8:1; 12:1; 16:1; 16:12).

2 Corinthians

Some time between the writing of 1 and 2 Corinthians, opponents of Paul had infiltrated the church in Corinth. Hence, the tone of 2 Corinthians is more defensive. Evidently, part of the strategy of these opponents was to call into question Paul's claim to be an apostle, perhaps because of his lack of demonstration of the power of the Spirit and his chronic suffering. They, on the other hand, were claiming to have lofty spiritual experiences and were promising the same to the Corinthians.

So Paul had a twofold task in 2 Corinthians. He had not only to provide a sustained defence of his apostleship, but also to persuade the Corinthians that his suffering did not undermine, but actually vindicated, the authority of his message. In 2 Corinthians we see Paul press home the paradoxical relationship between suffering and glory, death and resurrection, the

cross and the Spirit. In short, Paul is at pains to argue that his suffering, which his opponents took to be a strike against his legitimacy, actually serves as the very means by which the Spirit of God is poured out in the life of his churches, as the Corinthians themselves should be able to testify (2 Cor. 3:1–6).

Paul defends himself

Interestingly, Paul's self-defence begins with his explaining to the Corinthians the theological rationale for his change of travel plans (1:12–2:13). His change of plan may have caused them to doubt the sincerity of his intentions, or perhaps his opponents had capitalized on it as evidence of Paul's false motives.

From 2:14 to 7:16, Paul engages in an elaborate and subtle defence of his apostleship, appealing to suffering and the ministry of the Spirit, as well as the example of Moses and the Law (3:7–18).

Chapters 8 and 9 seem to represent a significant shift in the direction of the letter, as Paul turns to the issue of the collection for the Jerusalem church. But this pastoral admonition is perhaps not as out of place as it might perhaps at first appear. Paul knows that the measure of the Corinthians' trust in God will be reflected in their concern for other believers.

In 10:1–13:10 Paul mounts his most forceful attack against his detractors in Corinth who, though they claim to be 'servants of righteousness', are in fact 'false apostles' and 'deceitful workmen' (2 Cor. 11:12–15).

Together, the Corinthian letters stand as an abiding witness to Paul's theologically-driven pastoral practice with his newly-established churches.

Paul's Life

Approx. dates	Events	Letters	Main message
5	Born in Tarsus		
35	Converted on the road to Damascus		
35	Ministry in Arabia and Damascus (Galatians 1:17)		
38	Visit to Jerusalem after conversion (Acts 9:26; Galatians 1:18)		
38	Ministry in Syria and at home in Tarsus (Acts 11:25; Galatians 1:21)		
43	Ministry in Antioch with Barnabas Journey to Jerusalem (Acts 11:26–30)		
47	First missionary journey, then Council in Jerusalem (Acts 13–15)		
50	After 1st missionary journey	Galatians	Christ the liberator: freedom from the Law
50	During 2nd missionary journey, probably from Corinth (Acts 18:11)	1 & 2 Thessalonians	Christ the coming judge and Saviour
52	During 3rd missionary journey, from Ephesus (Acts 19:8–10)	1 & 2 Corinthians	Christ the law-giver for the church, his body
55	From Corinth (Acts 20:3)	Romans	Christ – God's way of salvation for Jew and Gentile alike
56	Journey to Jerusalem: arrested (Acts 21:1–23:35.)		
56	Imprisonment in Caesarea Journey to Rome (Acts 24–28)		
59	Ministry and imprisonment in Rome (Acts 28:30–31)	Ephesians, Philippians, Colossians, Philemon	Christ the Lord of the universe and of the church (Ephesians, Colossians); Christ the giver of joy in suffering (Philippians)
61	Release from captivity (Philippians 1:25; Philemon 22)		
61	Ministry in Asia Minor & Greece	1 Timothy, Titus	Life and ministry within the church of Christ
65	Rearrested, tried and martyred in Rome	2 Timothy	Guarding the faith by word and example

Part of the site of ancient Corinth.

A Theological Letter: Romans

Romans is widely regarded as Paul's most theologically significant letter. It would be hard to overstate the influence of this letter upon subsequent Christian thought and practice. Little wonder Romans has often been thought of as a compendium of Christian doctrine. Luther, in fact, said that Romans should be memorized word-for-word and pondered every day.

Why did Paul write Romans?

Paul probably had several reasons for writing Romans.

1. As we learn from 15:18–24, Paul was intent on preaching the gospel in Spain and planned to use the church in Rome as a support base for his mission westwards. Romans serves as an introduction and summary of Paul's gospel and mission.
2. Several passages suggest that Paul may have felt it necessary to provide some defence of his gospel (see 1:16; 3:8; 9:1–6). But to whom? Perhaps to the Roman Christians themselves, which might explain Paul's lengthy presentation of his 'credentials' in the letter opening (1:1–15). It is also possible that he wanted to enlist the Roman Christians to support him when he returned to Jerusalem, where he expected more serious questions about his understanding of his gospel and mission (see Acts 21–22). The irenic tone of the letter suggests that Paul desired to win over some whom he may have alienated, in particular by his handling of issues related to Jews – contrasting with the letter to the Galatians, where he seems to speak more negatively on these issues.
3. A careful reading of Romans 14:1–15:6 (see also 11:17–24) reveals that the church in Rome was experiencing some internal divisions or tensions. Students of this letter continue to discuss the precise nature of the issues at stake, in particular, the identity of the 'weak' and the 'strong' (14:1; 15:1). While the details remain unclear, we may safely assume that some more conservative members of the congregation, who were perhaps Jewish, took issue with the more

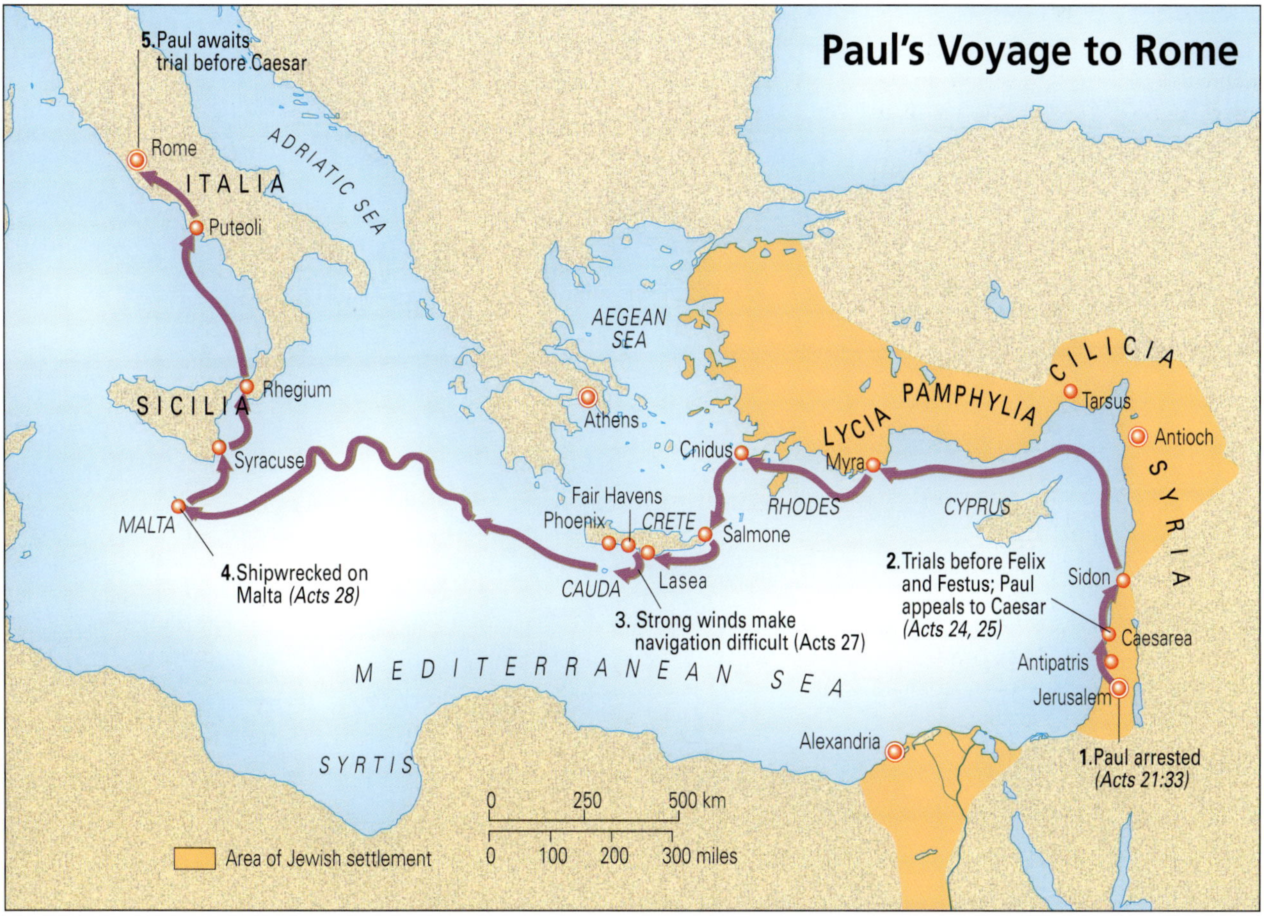

liberal practices of probably the majority of Christians in Rome on issues such as diet (14:2–3) and calendar observance (14:5–6). Paul probably intended Romans to quell some of these disputes.

What is Romans about?

Romans is ultimately about the gospel. This is clear from the statement in 1:16: 'For I am not ashamed of the gospel, for it is the power of God for salvation to everyone who believes, to the Jew first and also to the Greek.'

Inasmuch as Romans is about the gospel, it is also about the righteousness of God, as Paul clarifies in 1:17: 'For in [the gospel] the righteousness of God is revealed from faith for faith, as it is written, "The righteous shall live by faith."' This is the gospel promised beforehand in the 'Law and the Prophets' (3:21), the righteousness of God now revealed in the person and work of Christ and available to all believers, whether Jew or Gentile, on the basis of faith (3:21–26).

Romans serves as a grand exposition of the righteousness of God: in justification by faith (chapters 1–4), in the new life of obedience (chapters 5–8), in God's purposes with Israel and the nations (chapters 9–11) and in the new community gathered around the gospel (chapters 12–15).

While the righteousness of God is certainly the dominant theme of Romans, there is another important theme that weaves its way through the entire letter. The gospel not only reveals the righteousness of God, it also engenders hope.

In Romans, God is the God of hope (15:13) as well as the God of

The Roman Forum, once the centre of the Roman Empire.

the gospel (1:16–17). The scriptures produce hope (15:4); Abraham exemplifies hope (4:18); hope does not disappoint because the love of God has been shed abroad in our hearts (5:5); the creation was subjected to futility in hope (8:20); believers are to rejoice in hope (12:12). Ultimately, in fact, as Paul says, we are saved 'in hope' (8:24), and so Paul prays that the Holy Spirit will fill the Roman Christians with hope (15:12). Paul's letter to the Romans brims with confidence in the hope-giving power of the gospel of God's righteousness.

The ancient Colosseum, Rome.

Paul's Prison Letters:

Ephesians, Philippians, Colossians & Philemon

Ephesians, Philippians, Colossians and Philemon are often referred to as 'prison epistles'. Many of Paul's theological and practical exhortations to churches and individuals were forged on the anvil of persecution and suffering. These four letters were hammered out during a ministry stretching from Syria to Italy, beset by trials and dangers, yet yielding spiritual fruit in the establishment of many churches.

In these remarkable letters Paul both exemplifies and calls his readers to profound praise. With the conversion of every sinner, in the growth of his churches and even in extreme trial, Paul's proclamation of Christ's person and work stands forth.

Ephesians

To the church at Ephesus, Paul writes to ground and motivate worthy communal conduct accomplished through the activity of the Son and Spirit to the glory of God. The opening chapters reveal the grandeur of Christ's redemptive work for sinners and its impact on the community of faith (chapters 1–2). A new order for social, racial, family and economic relationships follows from their new status as members 'one of another' (4:25).

Further, their communal conduct is now to be marked by the presence and activity of the Spirit (5:15–21). The Spirit provides a dynamic and harmonious sphere of relationships in the church and equips the community with the power to face the spiritual forces of evil (chapter 6).

Colossians

In Colossians many of these same themes and exhortations appear. General encouragement to new-creation conduct in church and family relationships forms the heart of the letter. Colossians, however, contains more situation-specific details than its close cousin, Ephesians. For example, Paul mentions specific travel plans (4:7–9) and individual people (4:10–17).

As to the thrust of this letter, despite his various trials, Paul still earnestly desires faithfulness in the community at Colossae (1:3–13, 24–2:5). However, all his struggles against the deceptive and demonic cultural forces would be ineffectual without the clear confession of Christ which alone can accomplish this task. With joyful expectation, Paul stresses the reality of Christ's sovereign power (1:15–23) and salvation (2:20–23).

Artist's impression of Onesimus with his master, Philemon.

Site of ancient Philippi.

The Library of Celsus, Ephesus.

Site of the jail in Philippi in which Paul and Silas were probably imprisoned.

Philippians

To the Philippians, Paul sets out something of the marvellous mystery of Christ's humility and glory in accomplishing salvation for believers. Following Christ, the believers in Philippi are to become partakers, with Paul, of the gospel. The apostle's own identity and ministry is subsumed into the wonder of the crucified and risen Lord (3:1–11). This community, dear to Paul's own heart, ought to celebrate the advancement of the gospel, despite the suffering that came to Paul, Timothy, Epaphroditus and their other beloved ministers. Hence, Paul's call to 'rejoice' (4:4, 10).

Philemon

While known as the letter to Philemon, this letter is also addressed to Apphia and Archippus. Philemon, however, receives special attention because his former slave, Onesimus, has come to faith through Paul's ministry.

In this letter, Paul subtly – and not so subtly – directs Philemon into a new form of relationship with Onesimus. For a first-century Roman master and servant relationship has now to be re-oriented around their more fundamental relationship as fellow believers and members of the same family of faith (vv. 15–16). Thus, Paul can appeal to the ministry of the gospel in defence of Onesimus, who most likely left his master while still a non-believer. This short letter highlights Paul's concern for gospel-oriented relationships rather than maintenance of the cultural status quo.

Letters to Pastors:
1 & 2 Timothy, Titus

Approaching the end of his life, Paulsends pastoral care and correction to his principle co-workers and fellow church- planters. 1 and 2 Timothy and Titus convey personal and practical ministerial advice, together with exhortations and instruction against the dangers of heresy in the churches.

While these churches have grown in their understanding of, and obedience to, Christ, persecution from without and internal defections from within have also grown. The menace of false doctrine poses the greatest danger for the community and demands orthodox teaching and conduct. Therefore, these letters give specific advice to Timothy and Titus to fortify them and their churches in their struggle to preserve the faithful worship of Christ.

1 Timothy

Paul's first letter to Timothy begins and ends with godly admonition to uphold sound doctrine (1:3–11; 6:11–21). For Paul, this doctrine shapes the character of both the individual and the community, motivated by love and 'sincere faith' (1:5). Paul's own life is testimony to the transformative power of Christ's truth (1:12–17) and becomes an example to encourage Timothy in his ministry (1:18–20).

Paul gives instructions for members of the church (chapter 2) and for the leaders of the church (chapter 3). As a community, they are to co-operate with God's plan of redemption in Christ (2:1–7), and display that salvation in their conduct (2:8–15). As leaders – both elders and deacons – they are to embody in their lives the purity of the doctrine they teach (3:1–13). These church offices form the centre of Paul's instruction to Timothy, and are followed by an emphatic affirmation of the Christian confession (3:14–16).

For Paul, the church is a divine stronghold against demonic forces and deception. Therefore, Paul warns Timothy to perceive rightly the nature of the present conflict (4:1–10), and perceive truly his spiritual gifting (4:11–16). These general admonitions are given specific application with provisions for widows (5:3–16), elders (5:17–25) and slaves (6:1–2). Paul concludes this first pastoral letter by highlighting the vanity of false doctrine (6:3–10) and exhorting Timothy, his child in the faith, to the unswerving confession of Christ with which he has been entrusted.

View from the top tiers of the great theatre of Ephesus.

2 Timothy

2 Timothy, probably Paul's final letter, is written from a Roman prison. It is full of pastoral pathos and delivers a strong charge, like the final words of a coach before the big game. Paul reminds Timothy of his own witness and allegiance to the gospel (1:8–14). Moreover, he sets before Timothy's eyes the glory of the crucified and risen Christ (2:8–13), who is the content of the gospel that has been entrusted to him (2:8). Timothy's ministry is authenticated by the Spirit of God (1:7, 14), and must therefore propel the training of other men in authentic ministry (2:14–26).

Paul's admonitions to Timothy to pursue this faithful ministry proceed out of the witness of his own sufferings and toil for the gospel (3:10–13; 4:6–8). He also perceives the future suffering and godless opposition which Timothy will have to face (3:1–9; 4:3–4), including heretical teaching from those who are already 'swerving from the truth' (2:17–18).

To meet these challenges, Timothy's life and ministry must be saturated in the sacred scriptures, so that he may 'reprove, rebuke and exhort' (4:2). It is the Word of God which, above all other counsel, will equip Timothy to follow in Paul's footsteps and assure a faithful fight and safe journey to the glorious day of the Lord's appearing (4:6–8). Paul concludes the letter with petitions echoing his personal need and his commitment to the gospel, despite fierce opposition (4:9–22).

Titus

Paul's third pastoral epistle is to Titus. Paul provides Titus with words of wisdom and gives training for the continued nourishment of believers in Crete, offering advice similar to the instructions given to Timothy. Paul left Titus to 'appoint elders' for the Cretan churches (1:5), and now he reassures Titus, who is encountering opposition from legalists in the Christian community. Titus' ministry must include the stern rebuke of both pagan and empty religious practices (1:10–16), as well as instruction in 'sound doctrine' (2:1). Titus' conduct must be a 'model of good works' (2:7), for both believers as well as opponents (2:8; 3:8).

To safeguard the continuance of truth in the Christian communities of Crete, Paul specifies the role and character of the overseers (1:7–9). Likewise, the elderly, young and slaves all have specific tasks for nourishing the community (2:1–14). Avoiding controversy, Titus must ensure the godly conduct of the church, which is expectantly hoping for the appearance of 'the goodness and loving kindness of God [their] Saviour' (3:4).

Sources of Paul's Theology

Paul's theology did not arise in a vacuum. A number of different sources influenced his thinking and vision of who God is and what Christ has done. Paul's theology is like a river fed by several tributaries, which together give his thinking its direction and force.

Revelation

The most decisive influence on Paul's thinking was his encounter with the risen and glorified Christ on the road to Damascus as a result of which Paul realized that Jesus of Nazareth was God's anointed Son, Israel's long-awaited King, the Messiah. This encounter radically changed the direction of his life from persecutor of the faith to willing martyr (see Gal. 1:13–23).

As we have seen, Paul, along with other Jews at the time, may have viewed Jesus' crucifixion as evidence that he was under God's curse (see Gal. 3:13; Deut. 21:23). But his confrontation with the resurrected Christ completely dashed this possibility. Paul now understood that Jesus was the Son of God, the fulfilment of Israel's expectations, and therefore the Lord of history.

Scripture

A careful reading of Paul's letters reveals how indebted he was to the Bible of his day, the Old Testament (see, for example, Romans chapters 4; 9–11; Galatians 3; 1 Corinthians 10). Paul was a remarkable student of scripture and refers or alludes to the Old Testament on virtually every page of every letter.

As part of his Jewish upbringing and rigorous Pharisaic training, Paul developed a mastery of the scriptures, which not only significantly shaped his own thinking, but also assisted him in communicating the truth about the gospel to his churches. For it is likely that even his Gentile converts, many of whom attended the Jewish synagogue, where the scriptures were regularly read and expounded (see Acts 13:43, 50; 16:14; 17:4, 17; 18:7), would have had some acquaintance with the Jewish scriptures.

The life and teachings of Jesus

It is also clear that Paul drew significant inspiration from the life and teachings of Jesus. While he rarely quotes the words of Jesus explicitly (1 Cor. 7:10; 9:14; 11:23–24; see Acts 20:35), the basic pattern of Jesus' earthly life of faithfulness and self-sacrifice informs Paul's theology and his practical instruction of his churches.

Tradition and the first Christians

As important as the revelation of the risen Christ was for Paul's own understanding, not everything was received by direct revelation. For example, Paul refers to that which he has 'received' concerning the basic elements of the gospel (1 Cor. 15:3). As Paul readily acknowledges, others came before him, and we can safely assume that he gleaned much from his interaction with the other early Christians and, perhaps in particular, the Jewish believers in Jerusalem and Antioch.

Paul's letters show a variety of uses of early Christian liturgical materials, hymns and catechetical traditions. For example, Paul speaks of 'receiving' and 'delivering' traditions to his churches (1 Cor. 11:23; 15:3–11). In addition, some of Paul's moral instructions reflect traditional elements drawn from various sources: the Old Testament, popular philosophy and Jewish moral teaching (see Gal. 5:19–23).

Remains of the Capernaum synagogue.

God and Humanity

Artist's impression of Paul writing from a prison cell in Rome.

God was, of course, central to Paul's entire outlook. Yet Paul did not leave us with dry philosophical reflections on the nature of God, but with highly practical pastoral letters. As a result, nowhere do we find him reflecting systematically upon the nature of God. But his letters are permeated with numerous references to the work of God in history and salvation, which provide a basis for discussing what Paul thought about God.

Fallen humanity and God's wrath

We cannot fully appreciate Paul's insight into the redemption available in Christ without first understanding his analysis of the human predicament. The opening chapters of Romans paint a bleak picture of humanity, at least regarding the possibility of finding a way to salvation with God (1:18–3:20). As Paul makes plain, left to its own devices, humanity would go from bad to worse (1:21–32), only in the end to meet the wrath of divine judgement (1:18; 2:6–11; 3:9–20).

From Paul's perspective, humanity fell when Adam fell (see Rom. 5:12–20). Fallen humanity now has a predisposition towards evil which manifests itself in every manner of evil action (see Eph. 2:1–3).

More than this, Paul understands humanity as being held captive to various cosmic agents and powers. At the head of this list, of course, is Satan, who Paul refers to as 'the god of this age' (2 Cor. 4:4, NIV). He reminds the Ephesians that believers 'do not wrestle against flesh and blood, but against the rulers, against the authorities, against the cosmic powers over this present darkness, against the spiritual forces of evil in the heavenly places' (6:12). In his letters, Paul singles out three powers for repeated mention: sin, the flesh and death. Intriguingly, each of these is regularly personified as a cosmic actor or agent (see Rom. 5:12; 8:3; Gal. 3:22; 5:16–21).

Abraham and the promise

What did Paul believe about God? For Paul, God was not some abstract concept or impersonal force. The God to whom Paul refers is none other than the God of Abraham, Isaac and Jacob, the God of Israel, the God who raised Jesus Christ from the dead. For Paul, God has acted in history to reveal himself to his people, and ultimately in and through his Son, Jesus Christ. The God who called Abraham and redeemed Israel from Egypt is the same God who now has revealed himself in Jesus of Nazareth. In fact, Paul can speak of Abraham having had the gospel preached beforehand to him (see Gal. 3:8; Rom. 4). Passages like these reveal that God has been acting consistently and purposefully throughout redemptive history.

Israel and the Law

God's election of a particular people, Israel, to whom belong the covenants, the patriarchs, the giving of the Law and more besides (see Rom. 9:4–5), has an important bearing on Paul's perspective on God and humanity. Given the election of Israel, there were for Paul two kinds of people: Jews, who had the Law, and Gentiles, who did not (see Gal. 2:15; Rom. 2:12).

Yet one of the great affirmations of the Old Testament is the *Shema*, the pious Jewish confession that God is one, something Paul also embraces. This also had significant theological implications. In Romans 3:28–30, the oneness of God supports Paul's claim that God will justify Jews and Gentiles alike: 'For we hold that one is justified by faith apart from works of the law. Or is God the God of Jews only? Is he not the God of Gentiles also? Yes, of Gentiles also, *since God is one.*'

Jesus of Nazareth, Christ and Lord

If we were to identify a central conviction that shapes the rest of Paul's theology, it would be that Jesus is both Christ ('Messiah') and Lord. This belief impacts everything else Paul thinks.

Crucified and raised

As far as Saul the Pharisee was concerned, Jesus of Nazareth was rightly executed by the Romans as a criminal. This view, as we have seen, was completely shattered on the road to Damascus when Saul the Pharisee was confronted by the risen Jesus. As Paul says, through his resurrection, the earthly Jesus was 'declared to be the Son of God in power' (Rom. 1:4).

Jesus' resurrection served to vindicate him as God's anointed King. It also served as God's means of enthroning him as Lord over all creation and the church. So Paul can speak of only one God, and yet of Jesus Christ as himself Lord and as the one through whom all things exist (1 Cor. 8:6).

The gospel

Near the centre of Paul's theology is the gospel, his one word summary of what God has done in Christ Jesus to save and redeem a people for himself. The gospel (literally, 'good news') is for Paul ultimately a declaration of God's saving work brought about through the death and resurrection of Jesus Christ. As Paul reminds the Corinthians, the 'gospel' he preached is 'that Christ died for our sins in accordance with the scriptures, that he was buried, that he was raised on the third day in accordance with the scriptures, and that he appeared to Cephas, then to the twelve' (1 Cor. 15:3–4).

Paul was probably indebted to certain key Old Testament passages for his understanding of the gospel – in particular, Isaiah 40–66, where the language of gospel is used to describe the re-establishment of God's reign and rule over his people (Isa. 40:9; 52:7; 60:1–6; 61:1; see Rom. 10:15). Hence, he sometimes speaks of the 'gospel of God' (Rom. 1:1; 15:16); the gospel is God's gospel and it is about what God has done in Christ.

For Paul there is only one gospel and he is willing to defend its singularity at all costs (Gal. 1:6–9). But we must remember that the gospel is for both Jews and Gentiles alike (Gal. 2:11–16). Indeed, in Galatians Paul goes so far as to speak of the 'gospel to the uncircumcised' and 'to the circumcised' (i.e. to Gentiles and Jews, Gal. 2:7). And, as he says, he has been entrusted with the former: to preach the gospel among the Gentiles (Gal. 1:16; 2:7; Rom. 1:1–5).

In Christ

The phrases 'in Christ' or 'in the Lord' appear well over 100 times in Paul's letters. It was obviously an important concept for him. But what exactly does it mean to be 'in Christ' or 'in the Lord'? While it may be unwise to try to single out one particular interpretation, the phrase

Men and women mourn at the foot of the cross.

at least implies that believers find God's power at work in the person and work of Jesus Christ and among those who identify themselves with Jesus.

Paul uses the expression with different shades of meaning.

1. The means by which something is done: 'in Christ God was reconciling the world to himself' (2 Cor. 5:19).
2. The manner in which something is done: 'I am speaking the truth in Christ' (Rom. 9:1; 1 Cor. 15:58).
3. The place in which something happens (Eph. 2:6; 1 Cor. 15:21–22; see Col. 3:3–4).

The basic idea seems to be that 'in Christ' or 'in the Lord' is the sphere of God's saving power, the place where the risen Lord rules over his people.

Imitators of Christ

For Paul, Christ is indeed God and Lord, but in his earthly life and, in particular, his suffering and death, he provides believers with an example to follow. In several places Paul explicitly calls for believers to imitate Christ. Two aspects are held up for imitation.

1. Believers are to imitate Christ's self-giving service for the benefit of others (1 Cor. 11:1).
2. Christ is a model of endurance in the midst of suffering.

On several occasions, Paul appeals to the example of Christ as a means of either commending believers for their steadfastness in the midst of trials, or as a way of exhorting them to persevere in the face of opposition, as did Christ himself (1 Thess. 1:6–9; see 2:14).

Hence, Paul often appeals to the cross as a vivid metaphor for the kind of self-giving exemplified in the life of Christ and now, in turn, expected of believers. In fact, Paul refers to this as sharing in the sufferings of Christ (Phil. 3:10).

The Spirit and the Church

Christian experience and identity is initiated and defined by the presence and working of the Spirit. This was true for Paul as well as for the other New Testament writers.

The Spirit of God and of Christ

For Paul the Spirit is not some vague, ill-defined entity or mystical force. Rather, the Spirit is the Spirit of God and the Spirit of the Lord Jesus Christ (Rom. 8:9). The Spirit is a person, co-equal with both the Father and the Son (see 2 Cor. 13:14). We see in his letters that Paul ascribes to the Spirit the same kinds of things that he ascribes to both the Father and Jesus Christ.

The promised Spirit

One of the characteristic features of earliest Christianity was the conviction that the coming of the Spirit within their communities marked a significant turning-point in God's purposes in history. It signified the transition to a new age, a new era of saving history. As the New Testament writers make clear, this special outpouring of the Spirit was anticipated by the prophets, especially Isaiah (32:15; 44:3; 59:21), Ezekiel (11:19; 36:26) and Joel (2:28–32).

Paul refers to the Spirit as the 'promised Spirit' (Gal. 3:14; see Eph. 1:13), his shorthand way of referring to the fact that the dawning of the Spirit was predicted or 'promised' by the prophets of old. The book of Acts corroborates this point. As part of his Pentecost sermon, Peter proclaims: 'Being therefore exalted at the right hand of God, and having received from the Father the *promise of the Holy Spirit*, he has poured out this that you yourselves are seeing and hearing' (2:33).

The coming of the Spirit was doubly significant within early Christianity and, in particular, within Paul's own churches, because the Spirit was being poured out upon *Gentiles*. While this may not seem to us particularly significant, for the early Jewish believers this was very striking, as the story of Peter's encounter with Cornelius makes plain (see Acts 10:1–48; 11:1–18). And we find Paul appealing to the reception of the Spirit among the Gentiles, quite apart from the 'works of the Law', as a lynchpin in his argument with the Galatians (Gal. 3:1–5). For Paul, as well as for other early Christians, the presence of the Spirit was a sign of God's full acceptance.

The Spirit as down-payment

While the presence of the Spirit is a sign of the new age and a token of God's full acceptance, the Spirit's presence in the midst of the Christian community also points to the future. On a few occasions, Paul refers to the Spirit as the 'down-payment' of what is yet to come (2 Cor. 1:21–22; Eph. 1:14). What seems implied by this image is that the Spirit guarantees the reality of the believer's future inheritance and resurrection. Indeed, Paul says we have the 'first instalment' of that future inheritance, a foretaste of resurrection life in the Spirit (see

Rom. 7:6). For Paul, the Spirit prods us to look to the future, as we eagerly anticipate the redemption of our bodies (Rom. 8:18–27; 1 Cor. 15:42–49; Gal. 5:5).

The Spirit and the church

In Paul's understanding, the church is comprised of those who, through faith in the Lord Jesus Christ, have received the 'Spirit of adoption' (Rom. 8:15; Gal. 4:5–6) and as a result have been 'set apart' or 'sanctified' by the Spirit (1 Cor. 6:11). Believers thus share in the common experience of the Spirit: the Spirit's power, agency, ministry and gifts. It is this shared experience of the Spirit – what Paul refers to as being 'baptized' into the Spirit (1 Cor. 12:13) – that provides the basis for the unity of the church (Eph. 4:3) and for the fellowship of its members (2 Cor. 13:14; Phil. 2:1).

In several places Paul speaks of the 'gifts' of the Spirit (1 Cor. 12:4–31; see Rom. 12:4–8; Eph. 4:7–16). These are Spirit-empowered abilities, as Paul says, 'apportion[ed] to each one' as the Spirit wills (1 Cor. 12:11). They include wisdom, knowledge, healing, the working of miracles, prophecy, tongues, service, leadership, teaching and generosity (1 Cor. 12:8–10; Rom. 12:6–8). And they are intended, not to give individual believers a platform for boasting, a problem Paul faced in Corinth, but ultimately for building up the body as a whole (Eph. 4:12). As Paul says to the Corinthians: 'To each is given the manifestation of the Spirit for the common good' (1 Cor. 12:7).

The Christian Life and the Future

Paul's theology also made a very important place for Christian living, or ethics. Paul's ethics, in fact, were thoroughly theological, just as his theology was thoroughly ethical. What he believed about God, Christ and the Spirit had a direct bearing on how he thought believers should live.

Faith, hope and love

The triad of faith, hope and love frequently appears in Paul's letters, providing a convenient way of understanding the heart of Paul's vision of how believers are to live their new life in Christ. For Paul, faith is the defining feature of Christian living and the source of the believer's obedience. He speaks in Romans, for example, of 'the obedience that comes from faith' (1:5; cf. 16:26, NIV).

While faith is a more prominent term for Paul, hope is no less essential for a right understanding of his view of the Christian life. Because believers live between Christ's first and second coming, they necessarily live a life of hope.

As to love, one could hardly overstate its importance in Paul's view of the Christian life. Love is the cardinal virtue, without which nothing else counts. Paul underscores this eloquently in 1 Corinthians 13. For Paul, love is also chief among the 'fruit of the Spirit' (Gal. 5:22–23).

The believer and the Jewish Law

How should the believer now relate to the Jewish Law? This is an age-old question, with diverse and competing answers on offer. Paul, in step with Jesus, believed that love was the essence of the Law and thus that the believer's behaviour should be loving and reflect the essence of the Law (Gal. 5:14; Rom. 13:8–10).

But Paul says more: when believers serve one another in love, they actually 'fulfil' the Law (Gal. 5:13–14; Rom. 13:8–10; see Gal. 6:2). So while Paul obviously does not think Gentiles are obliged to take on Jewish rites to find full acceptance with God, he makes plain that as they walk by the Spirit, their lives will fully measure up to what the Law requires (Gal. 5:13–6:10).

The Spirit and new life

We would badly misrepresent Paul's teaching if we thought that the new life of the Christian was to be lived from his or her own resources. On the contrary, Paul insists that there is a powerful, effective agency making possible the new obedience of the Christian: that is, the Spirit.

We have already discussed the important place of the Spirit in Paul's theology; now it is time to stress how indispensable the working of the Spirit is for Paul's ethics. Paul uses two phrases, both found in Galatians, which help capture his thinking about the Spirit in relation to ethics.

First, Paul charges the Galatians: 'walk by the Spirit, and you will in no way fulfil the desire of the flesh' (5:16). Here we find the strongest possible assurance of the fact that walking by the Spirit enables the Christian community and the individual believer to avoid indulging the flesh and its works (see 5:19–21).

Just a few verses later, Paul speaks of being 'led by the Spirit' (5:18). There is, then, both a passive and active dimension to our interaction with the person and work of the Spirit. We are to walk by the Spirit (active), and yet we are to allow ourselves to be led by the Spirit (passive). Both are true, and both are essential dimensions of the new life of the Christian. For only when we rely completely upon the working of the Spirit will we be able to see the 'fruit of the Spirit' in our lives (5:22–23).

Final judgement

For Paul, the Christian life is to be lived in the light of the Day of the Lord, the return of Christ, when God will judge the world by Jesus Christ (Rom. 2:16; 1 Thess. 1:10). This is the awesome, impending reality that dominates Paul's horizon as he looks to the future, and in turn informs his conduct in the present.

As Paul explains to the Corinthians: 'So whether we are at home or away, we make it our aim to please him. For we must all appear before the judgement seat of Christ, so that each one may receive what is due for what he has done in the body, whether good or evil' (2 Cor. 5:9–10; see 1 Cor. 4:4–5). So, suggests Paul, believers should live in the light of that Day, by God's grace ordering their conduct aright, as they anticipate each one giving an account to God (see Rom. 14:10–12).

Resurrection and new creation

Paul set great stock by the fact that believers will experience a future, bodily resurrection. This was not an addendum to the faith, but in many ways the focal point of the believer's future hope. As Paul himself says: 'If in this life only we have hoped in Christ, we are of all people most to be pitied' (1 Cor. 15:19).

But Paul is confident that at the end of time, when the trumpet sounds, the dead in Christ 'will be raised imperishable' (1 Cor. 15:52). They will have experienced a profound change and, as Paul says, find their natural bodies giving way to spiritual, resurrection bodies (1 Cor. 15:42–49). After the final judgement, believers will be granted entrance into the 'new creation' (Gal. 6:15), the 'kingdom of God' (Gal. 5:21), that final, perfected state of being, where they will dwell with God and Christ for ever.

Paul's Legacy

We should perhaps not be surprised to discover that the complex life and ministry of Paul has aroused diverse and at times contradictory responses. Throughout church history, different people have seized on ambiguities or tensions in Paul's thinking and radicalized them in one direction or another. As a result, Paul's legacy is just as colourful as was his life.

Second-century Christians

Among some of the second-century Fathers of the church, Paul was known as *the* apostle to the Gentiles. He was also renowned for the nobility of his character. In fact, his remarkable perseverance was regarded as something to be emulated.

Clement of Rome, writing towards the middle of the second century, tells us:

> Seven times [Paul] was in bonds, he was exiled, he was stoned, he was a herald both in the East and in the West, he gained the noble fame of his faith, he taught justice to the whole world, and when he had reached the limits of the West he gave his testimony before the rulers, and thus passed from the world and was taken up into the Holy Place – the greatest example of endurance. (*1 Clement* 5.6–7).

Paul was also a favourite among certain heretical factions within early Christianity. Marcion, perhaps the best known among them, was very fond of Paul, taking some of Paul's letters as the core of his own restricted canon of scripture. At the other end of the spectrum, a Jewish Christian group known as the Ebionites reacted strongly to Paul's legacy, viewing him as the destroyer of the Law of Moses. Then there were the Gnostics, who stressed Paul as a miracle-worker and ascetic. Common to all of these heterodox portraits of the apostle is a fundamental imbalance: each keyed in to one particular strand of Paul's thinking to the exclusion of others, distorting his thinking as a whole.

Luther and the Reformation

Paul's letters rose to a place of prominence during the Protestant Reformation. Luther was very fond of Paul's writings, since he thought they promoted the gospel in its purest, most undiluted form. Moreover, the emergence of justification by faith alone as the central truth of Christian teaching during the Reformation helped secure Paul's place as the theologian of Protestantism.

The historical Paul and the modern era

During the eighteenth and nineteenth centuries, the study of Paul took on a more historical and less theological orientation. Scholars were less interested in Paul as a dogmatic theologian and defender of orthodox Christianity, and more interested in his place within the development of religious ideas at the turn of the millennium. Students of Paul became preoccupied with

The Appian Way, Rome. Paul walked this road as a prisoner on his way to Rome.

Karl Barth, whose important study of Romans (1919) helped break the dominant liberal theology of the West.

questions about the source and origin of Paul's ideas about God, Christ and humanity. This strong historical interest continues largely unabated into the present.

Paul in contemporary perspective

The study of Paul has been pursued with renewed intensity in recent years, with a new range of questions being asked and some fresh answers being offered. Students are now more aware than ever of the importance of Paul's Jewish background as the primary context for understanding his ministry, thought and self-understanding. Precisely what this means continues to be debated vigorously. In the end, however, Paul remains as fascinating and monumental a figure nearly two millennia on as he was during his own lifetime.

Further Reading

Bruce, F. F., *Paul: Apostle of the Heart Set Free* (Grand Rapids: Eerdmans, 1977). A classic introduction to the life and ministry of Paul by one of the leading conservative New Testament scholars of the twentieth century.

Dunn, James D. G., editor, *The Cambridge Companion to Saint Paul* (Cambridge: Cambridge University, 2003). A fine collection of essays covering Paul's life, thought and letters from various leading Pauline scholars.

Hawthorne, Gerald F., Ralph P. Martin & Daniel G. Reid, editors, *Dictionary of Paul's Life and Letters* (Downers Grove: IVP, 1993). A standard reference work with a wealth of information on practically every imaginable topic related to Paul.

Hooker, Morna D., *Paul: A Short Introduction* (Oxford: Oneworld, 2003). A useful introduction to Paul from a leading British Pauline scholar.

Ridderbos, Herman, *Paul: An Outline of His Theology* (Grand Rapids: Eerdmans, 1975). A classic introduction to Paul's theology.

Schreiner, Thomas, *Interpreting the Pauline Epistles* (Grand Rapids: Baker Academic: 1990). A very useful introduction to interpreting Paul's letters, though it assumes some knowledge of Greek.

Schreiner, Thomas, *Paul, Apostle of God's Glory in Christ: A Pauline Theology* (Downers Grove: IVP, 2001). A good introduction to Paul's theology using God's glory in Christ as the organizing theme.

Thielman, Frank, *Paul and the Law: A Contextual Approach* (Downers Grove: IVP, 1994). A very good, conservative introduction to the question of Paul and the Law.

Wenham, David, *Paul: Follower of Jesus or Founder of Christianity?* (Grand Rapids: Eerdmans, 1995). An accessible introduction to the question of Paul's relationship to Jesus.

Westerholm, Stephen, *Understanding Paul: The Early Christian Worldview of the Letter to the Romans* (Grand Rapids: Baker Academic, 2004). Provides a very good introduction to the presuppositions of Paul's thinking.

Witherington, Ben III, *Paul Quest: The Renewed Search for the Jew of Tarsus* (Downers Grove: IVP, 1998). A very useful introduction to the discussion of the historical Paul.

Wright, N. T., *Paul: In Fresh Perspective* (Minneapolis: Fortress, 2006). A highly readable and provocative presentation of Paul's theology by one of the world's leading New Testament scholars.

Ziesler, John, *Pauline Christianity* (New York: Oxford University, 1990). A concise and accessible introduction to Paul's life and thought.

Index

Published in 2011 by Kregel Publications, a division of Kregel, Inc., PO Box 2607, Grand Rapids, MI 49501.

ISBN: 978-0-8254-4197-4

Worldwide coedition produced by
Lion Hudson plc
Wilkinson House
Jordan Hill Road
Oxford OX2 8DR, England
Tel.: +44 (0) 1865 302750
Fax: +44 (0) 1865 302757
Email: coed@lionhudson.com
www.lionhudson.com

Printed in Singapore

Acknowledgments:
Photographs
Jon Arnold: pp. 6–7, 14–15, 18–19
Bridgeman Art Library: p. 5
Tim Dowley: p. 8, 10–11, 12, 13

Illustrations
Jeremy Gower: p. 3
Richard Scott: p. 20, 25, 26, 30